What Is Workplace Prayer?

A.J. Lykosh , Bob Perry

MAKARIOS
PRESS

Makarios Press

What the church needs today is not more machinery or better, not new organizations or more and novel methods, but men whom the Holy Spirit can use—men of prayer, men mighty in prayer. The Holy Ghost does not flow through methods, but through men. He does not come on machinery, but on men. He does not anoint plans, but men—men of prayer. ~ E.M. Bounds

Contents

Introduction

My parents, John and Sarita Holzmann, started the home-schooling company Sonlight Curriculum in 1990. At the time, they had already been mentored in prayer for some years. My dad had been on staff with a missions organization that had morning prayer every day as part of their staff responsibilities, as well as a 24-hour-a-day prayer room. Both parents would get up in the night about once a month to take their two-hour shift.

Because my parents talked to missionaries from around the world, and read numerous missionary biographies, they had a sense of how much of life is not only a physical, but a spiritual battle, too.

So when they started Sonlight, they started with prayer.

From its beginning, Sonlight has offered morning prayer to the staff: optional, on-the-clock prayer, available to any of the staff who choose to come.

The staff who accept the invitation pray for their customers, pray for their vendors, pray for the work of the day, and cover any specific requests from customers.

When the company turned 30, John and Sarita, along with me, my brother, and Sonlight's long-time general manager, spent some time reflecting over the goodness of God, celebrating what he has done in the company.

We hoped to get 30 testimonies.

Instead the list reached 60, and then kept going.

A double portion and more.

A few of the prayers were specific, smaller provisions, such as my distinct memory of a family friend telling her mom in the first year of business, "I would love to buy every book you sell, Sarita."

And then a donor offered to buy this woman all the school supplies she would need for two years. Since she had many children, all two years apart, she literally bought every book.

But most of the provisions were enormous in scope.

Sonlight sells a lot of books, and has survived the rise of Amazon.

A few more beautiful examples.

Sonlight had approximately 600 employees, cumulatively, over the first 30 years.

In those first 30 years, the Holzmanns report:

• We had one divorce, and it was amicable, and there were no children involved. One divorce across probably 400 or 500 marriages.

• We had one death: a spouse that survived half a decade or so longer than expected. We had a hard time thinking of even ten people or family members that have had a major health trial in 30 years of business.

• Of all the employees, commuting to work over the decades, we had one accident. And though her car was totaled, she herself was completely safe and came to work the next day.

• One more story: in 1997, at the height of our busy season, UPS went on strike.

We had no warning.

Later, our rep mentioned that she had been calling the companies in alphabetical order, and she hadn't reached "S." ("Oh! You're our largest customer in this region right now! Huh. Maybe I should have called you sooner.")

FedEx, in order to survive, wasn't taking new customers. The post office allowed each person to ship a very limited number of boxes, which meant that we could have mailed, at best, something like 26 packages total.

It was not a pretty picture. The boxes in the warehouse were stacking up, and our customers were getting more and more anxious.

In the scramble to come up with a plan, somebody remembered that some months before, FedEx had reached out: "Would you like a free overnight envelope?"

At the time, the staff person thought, *Maybe at some point, we will need to overnight a document. Then we'll have a free mailer.*

And because of that mailer, we had an account with FedEx. So, officially, we were clients, and they started shipping for us.

The list goes on: perfect timing, favorable loans, unexpected help, tremendous staff, creative thinking....[1]

God has been so good to the family, the staff, and the customers.

Clearly, God is not opposed to prayer in business.

He's not opposed to business people paying others to pray.

In fact, he blesses the prayers of the saints and he blesses the companies that value the prayers of the saints.

We invite you, too, to make prayer, and paid prayer, a foundation of your business.

---

1. You can find the whole list in the Appendix.

How We Work

Chapter 1

How We Work

Many churches have a worship leader, a paid staff member, who picks the music and runs the rehearsals and, perhaps, offers a brief meditation in the midst of the set.

That's a job. At least a part time, and sometimes a full time job: listening to music, not recycling the same songs year after year, writing original music.

When churches pay a worship leader, they're paying the worship leader for their time. The worship leader brings their training and their skill and the gifts that the Lord has given them.

Scripture tells of the paid worshippers during the Tabernacle of David period, and we understand that worship ministers have bills.

But when it comes to prayer, we don't have any context of what it looks like for somebody to be a prayer minister.

What does business intercession looks like?

Chapter 2

The "Prayer" Part of Workplace Prayer

A t Workplace Prayer, the leadership team prays for our clients as our full-time job.

• **Individual Prayer**

Bob once said to me that he prays in the Spirit constantly. Beautiful.

While I feel like I walk with the Holy Spirit at all times, I don't know that I quite pray constantly, but as the Lord leads. I aim for a minimum of an hour a day with just me and Jesus.

• **Partnership Prayer**

Bob and I pray together daily for at least an hour, and usually longer.

We believe this is one of our distinct advantages. Deuteronomy 32:30 says, "How could one man chase a thousand, or two put ten thousand to flight, unless their Rock had sold them, unless the LORD had given them up?"

What an advantage! Adding one additional person gives ten times the total result!

Prayer partnership makes a tremendous difference.

• **Corporate Prayer**

Bob and I treasure our larger intercessor team.

We count it a joy and privilege to pray with our team several times a week. These prayer partners help cover our clients in a variety of ways.

• **Fasting**

Both Bob and I fast regularly.

Bob has been fasting for decades. I started fasting weekly in July 2019, almost a year before I met him.

In some seasons, the Lord asks us to fast a couple of days a week. In other seasons, maybe only once.

Several times a year, we invite our larger community to participate in corporate fasts with us. We do 21-day fasts in January and August,[1] and shorter fasts a few other times a year.

We love fasting because of the amazing promises in Isaiah 58:6-12, including:

- Loose the chains of injustice and untie the cords of the yoke.

- Set the oppressed free.

---

1. Not necessarily water-only!

- Break every yoke.

- Satisfy your needs in a sun-scorched land.

- Strengthen your frame.

At Workplace Prayer, we don't know how God will work in any given scenario.

But however God works, we are standing in the gap, in faith.

We pray for you, your family, and your business.

For Bob, prayer has been the passionate study of his lifetime. For me, prayer has been a part of my life since childhood.

Prayer is our privilege, our vocation, and our passion.

And it is for our larger team as well.

Chapter 3

Practically, How Does This Work?

When people partner with Workplace Prayer, we send out an intake form.

Some of our clients never fill out the intake form. We still pray for them. They still see results.

Richard Koch talks about the importance of *Simplify*, to allow a client or customer to have the easiest possible experience.

John McGee said, "You are the ultimate simplify company. People pay, and they literally don't need to do another thing."

True.

But most of our clients fill out the intake form and send that back to us.

This intake form offers the baseline of what the client is hoping for.

We welcome all requests. Business requests, personal requests.

We believe that God has a solution for everything, so we don't have boundaries around what we pray for and what we don't.

Some people feel comfortable sharing very personal challenges.

Some share a few general bullet points.

There's not a right or wrong way to share requests.

As we pray, oftentimes we find that we're praying not only on the micro level, for our specific people and their businesses, but also on the macro level, for the broad concerns of the day.

For example, one week, as we talk to different clients, we find that they are all oddly weary.

Another week, their thinking feels foggy.

Another week, everything seems to be breaking.

Another week, the voice of the accuser keeps telling them their input is unwelcome.

Another week, financial challenges seem to be squeezing in more than normal.

I don't know why these sorts of things come in waves, but they do.

So we pray at both the micro level and the macro level.

After the intake form, we welcome our people to send us requests, as they choose.

In truth, most people don't do this.

As a client myself, I have a reminder on my calendar, so I send a quick email every week: "These are my praises from last week; this is what I'm sensing for this next week."[1]

Other clients update us monthly.

Some clients text us occasionally. "I'm heading into a big meeting with the attorney in 15 minutes. Please pray."

In general, we get far less updates than I initially expected.

But I appreciate that we pray, whether we get updates or not.

God knows the cries of our hearts, and he answers.

---

1. See appendix for a sample.

Chapter 4

We Welcome All Requests

Although the name of our business is Workplace Prayer, the reality is: no business owner is just a business owner.

Business owners are also fathers and mothers and parents and siblings and children and friends. We are *people*.

As part of our role as intercessors, seeking the Lord on behalf of our clients, we don't just want prayer requests about their businesses. Each one is a complete person.

And so we want to know, to the extent that each is comfortable sharing, requests beyond the business.

Bob suggests our clients could think through prayer requests in three parts.

1) The business part. Whatever is needed.

2) The personal part. You, your spouse, your family, your friends.

3) Your clients, customer, or community. What larger picture needs do you see?

We want the ripple effect of God's kingdom advance not to stop with our clients, but to go on to the people that we serve.

Chapter 5

We Love Big Requests

Once I was talking to a client about some of his goals and dreams for the next year. I enjoyed the conversation, full of so much big picture thinking.

Suddenly he said, "Is it okay if I ask for these things? Can I actually just say what I want? I don't know if I've ever voiced these desires of my heart. It's almost scary to speak them aloud."

What beautiful honesty.

I suspect that many of us have a tendency to restrict our ask, because we don't want to seem greedy.

Here are two answers to this concern.

First, the New Testament answer.

In Philippians 2:13, we read "For God is working in you, giving you the desire and the power to do what pleases him."[1]

In other words, because God is working in us, he forms both our desires and our ability to accomplish them.

As we walk with God, we can embrace the things that God has put on our hearts, because he gave us the desire to begin with.

But what if we have a desire that isn't God-given?

We pray, as Epaphras did for the church at Colossae, "that ye may stand perfect and complete in all the will of God."[2]

God is able to prune our desires, as needed.

Second, the Old Testament answer.

My natural tendency is to ask bigger for others, and smaller for myself.

Bob's tendency is to ask big for everyone and everything. He even has a "PRAY BIG" sign in his office.

Bob taught me to pray the prayer of Jabez. He started praying I Chronicles 4:10 back in 1983, 17 years before the famous *Prayer of Jabez* came out.

Jabez cried out to the God of Israel, "Oh, that you would bless me and enlarge my territory! Let your hand be with me, and keep me from harm so that I will be free from pain." And God granted his request.

---

1. NLT

2. Colossians 4:12

Jabez asked for blessing and influence, for protection and comfort.

And the verse doesn't end with, "And God, angered, smote Jabez for asking for too many blessings."

No. Jabez prayed a big prayer, "And God *granted* his request."

God said yes.

Do you go around asking the Lord to bless you?

Do you ask for more influence?

Do you ask for protection? (As any investor knows, it's so terribly important not to lose the gains you've earned.)

Do you ask for comfort?

If you have some desire in your heart, voice it.

When you partner with the Workplace Prayer team, we welcome your big prayers.

We'll even take your big prayers and add to them.

So: what is it that you want in the next season of your life? You have permission to actually just say, "This is what I want."

And then pray for it.

Chapter 6

What Coverage Looks Like

When my family first hired Bob, I wanted to know: does our family have an assigned prayer time?

I had a friend hire me to pray for her business, back before I partnered with Bob, and she paid for one hour a month.

Bob had such a fascinating answer.

He said, "When you hire me, I carry you all month. Not just for an hour."

Today we sometimes hear this question phrased a bit differently: "Do you pray for me specifically? Or am I part of a blanket prayer?"

We do pray for our clients by name. We treasure each of them, and their businesses and enterprises.

But we don't say, "Here is the hour to pray for this one client."

That wouldn't be enough coverage!

The Workplace Prayer leadership team prays prayers of protection and cutting free every morning. We pray together about whatever things the Lord puts on our hearts, and often we find that the places we need breakthrough are also places our clients need breakthrough.

We welcome prayer requests at any time, whether through email or text.

To me, as a paying client, I appreciate that I don't have one hour of prayer coverage a month, but a constant umbrella of protection.

Chapter 7

Weekly Prayer Calls

O n Tuesdays, it's our privilege, as the Prayer Advocate team, to spend time in prayer, along with any clients who are able to join us.

Many clients aren't able to join us regularly, but even an occasional call can be helpful, as this client wrote after joining us for the first time.

*

Since we did not have our weekly team meeting this morning, I was able to jump on the Workplace Prayer call.

Even though I had to answer a phone call in the middle of the meeting, and even though I arrived a bit late, being on the call this morning was something like:

Floating along in a refreshing river

Every time someone shared a verse and prayed out of it

There was a new wave—a new rise in the water

I come out of this prayer call with a much higher level of the activated Word flowing in me

Thank you again for stewarding this stream

*

Yes. Amen.

After being part of tens of thousands of prayer calls (!), Bob developed a unique method. Simple enough that even first time pray-ers can participate; rich enough that experienced people of prayer continue to find refreshment.

Chapter 8

Weekly Blessings

A s Bob prays through the week, he pays attention to the overall direction of his prayers. Though we pray together seven days a week, but he often comes out of the weekend with a specific burden of prayer.

We send out that prayer weekly to our Workplace Family.

Below you can find an example.[1]

———ele———

Ephesians 1:18 (NLT). "I pray that your hearts will be flooded with light so that you can understand the confident hope he has given to those he called—his holy people who are his rich and glorious inheritance."

Lord, I pray for the Workplace Prayer community, that the eyes of our hearts will be enlightened, so we may know the

---

1. From October 18, 2022

hope of our call. I ask for hope and optimism, but yet also focus and clarity.

Lord, I pray for biblical, foundational hope, which can make us optimistic like a farmer, ready to plant some seeds. And, Lord, if I water the seeds, and the conditions are right, they will grow and yield a harvest.

Father, I do pray, like it says in the Amplified Version, "And [I pray] that the eyes of your heart [the very center and core of your being] may be enlightened [flooded with light by the Holy Spirit], so that you will know *and* cherish the hope [the divine guarantee, the confident expectation] to which He has called you, the riches of His glorious inheritance in the saints (God's people)."

Lord, impart the hope found in your word. Break the waves of hopelessness; break the waves of pessimism; break the waves of depression.

Lord, John 10:10 says that the thief comes to steal, kill, and destroy, but Jesus comes to give life abundantly.

You come to give us hope and a future.

For the places where we are weary—whether due to the supply chain, or not having staff, or not having staff who work with a good will, or anything else—Lord, we speak strengthening.

Lord, for any wayward child, we ask that any such children return to you.

Lord, we pray for the finances.

Where we are discouraged and frustrated and weary, Lord, give us encouragement. Give us hope. In Jesus' name, Amen.

Chapter 9

Prophet, Priest, and King

Almost from the beginning of Workplace Prayer, we have wanted to give our clients prophetic words, insight from the Lord to help us on our way.

The Old Testament lists three offices: prophet, priest, and king. Mike Thakur, in *Mike Drop*, argues convincingly that business leaders fulfill the role of king: in many places, business leaders control more money than many kings of old.

At Workplace Prayer, we believe we operate, in a modern context, as priests. The Lord has given us grace to pray.

We each have our role. For those with the gift to pray, we need to pray.

The Lord was very clear with us: our role is to pray for business to get results. Pray for breakthrough.

But we didn't want to stop with only a king and a priest. We wanted the third function, that of prophet.

In the Old Testament, prophets proclaimed truth and revealed God's plans for the future.

In the New Testament, Paul wrote, "But the one who prophesies speaks to people for their strengthening, encouraging and comfort."[1]

Both Bob and myself have been quite blessed by the prophetic words we've received. They have strengthened, encouraged, comforted. Some of them clarify our identity. Some of them offer direction.

One of our clients told us about a specific prophetic word that was encouraging in a dark time.

Usually we like encouraging words, but in this particular word, he received a line about "There would be a loss."

Later that month, the family dog of 16 years died. As they were burying their dog, sad about the loss of this longtime companion of the family, all of a sudden one of them realized: "This is the loss!"

And as odd as it sounds, it was so comforting for them. The Lord knew what was coming, and he was still there, walking with them.

To clarify, though: our team prays over the names and seeks to hear, sense, or see what the Lord is speaking. They do this independently.

Occasionally, a client will ask, "What are you seeing for us?"

---

1. I Corinthians 14:3

We don't usually offer much in response, as this feels too much like a Magic-8 Ball prayer: shake the ball and get an answer from the expert.

No.

We view our role in prayer as keeping the channel open for you to see for yourself, to hear from God and have clarity enough to move forward with a reasonable amount of confidence, a reasonable degree of certainty.

We do come alongside our clients in various ways, but we view ourselves in a support role, not an authoritative role.

The Lord gave each client a role, a dream, a place, and we are happy to celebrate and support each one in the pursuit of the Lord's fullness.

Chapter 10

Two Favorite Functions of Workplace Prayer

In April 2023, Bob and I gave a lunch presentation at the Heaven in Business annual national conference.

Coming out of that time, I said, "Bob, you made everybody feel so cared for! You have such a heart of compassion, and people in the room all felt loved."

And Bob said,

> You made everybody feel cheered. As they walked in, you were cheering, "Yay, Sharon! Yay, Lonnie! Welcome, welcome!"
>
> I think that this is part of what we do at Workplace Prayer. We care and we cheer.
>
> Yes, of course we pray.

But we're a cheerleader for others' dreams. We want to hold them up, strengthen them, encourage them.

And part of the call to pray for a business is also to say, "We celebrate the call of God on your life, and we are excited to partner with you to bring that call to fulfillment."

I liked this observation.

When people come to visit me, I cheer for them. I live 45 minutes out of town, and I feel like anyone who makes the effort to come see me should get at least a cheer.

But I have another reason beyond that.

When I think about my childhood, I think of my mother coming to every athletic event and cheering for me. Birthday parties every year with friends who celebrated me. Various certificates, medals, and trophies: AWANA, athletics, scholastic.

But as an adult, after wedding showers and baby showers, the next celebratory party most of us can expect is (perhaps) a 50th birthday surprise party.

The reality of adulthood: not only do we have more responsibilities and more history (including, for most of us, more painful parts), but we often have fewer life-giving voices speaking into our lives.

We don't have enough cheers.

If you are in need of more cheering, or more care, this is part of what we seek to do.

Some Benefits

Chapter 11

Some Benefits

Why pay someone to pray for you and your business?

Bob wrestled with this question for years. Most of his life, he prayed for people and ministries for free.

He said, "I thought it was my duty to pray. And then, especially when I met my friend Paul Van Hoesen, he said, 'Bob, your prayers really make a difference. When you come and pray with me and with my company, we see measurable results. When we started praying together, we saw a real impact.' That changed my mind. Prayer is something that should be compensated and rewarded."

Here are some of the benefits you can expect when you have a strategic prayer partnership.

Chapter 12

Someone Has Your Back

After clients partner with us, we can't predict what will happen. Each client experiences different things.

But the most common comment we hear from them is that they feel like someone actually has their back ... maybe for the first time.

We often also see their staff shuffle around, so that the right people fill the right roles.

Often the cash flow situation starts to turn around, or open up more thoroughly.

Often they have new and creative ideas.

Or they find new and unexpected partners.

Full Disclosure: not all the changes feel good. It's not fun to find out that your partner has been planning a hostile takeover, or that your wife has a brain tumor.

But in those situations, what was hidden came to light. That, too, is a gift.

Whether the situation is good or bad, though, we cover in prayer.

Chapter 13

Return on Investment

When Bob and I started Workplace Prayer, we asked the Lord about the ROI on a regular basis.

Lord, we think that praying for business is a good idea. We think that it will work. We think that this is a need in the body of Christ.

But we recognize these are business people, and, for the most part, if they don't see a return on investment, they are not going to keep paying us.

Over the years, we have been delighted to find that, yes, prayer, *in aggregate*, actually does produce results.

That said, we can't guarantee what the Lord will do.

Some clients do get an absolutely astonishing financial ROI.

For one of our first clients, I prayed that he would have 100x in new business for every dollar he invest with us. A year in,

I asked him about the dollar figure. "Oh! It ended up being more like 142x!" he said.

Some clients hold steady.

Some don't improve much at all, or are in a field that isn't as profitable today as it once was. (The tech world, especially, changes quickly.)

My friend and Workplace Prayer Advocate Andrew said,

> ROI is not only measured only in increase, but it can also be measured in not having additional loss when things are going sideways in your industry. It could also mean that your supply chain is solid, your inventory is sufficient for the increased sales, your logistics and shipping partners down the line are highly efficient so that delivery of your products and services are on time, that your products arrive safe and not damaged.
>
> There are so many dimensions to ROI than just the above, and I haven't even gotten to team and culture.

Chapter 14

Measurable Results

A strategic prayer partnership provides measurable results not only in business but in the rest of your life as well.

How are you wounded? Rocky marriage? Wayward children? Recurrent tendency to sin? Persistent illness? Susceptibility to depression?

When you hire a person to pray for you and your business, you'll see progress in your life, in the lives of your families, and in your professional development.

Prayer brings greater peace in your home, which frees you to be able to function more clearly in your role at work.

And since your personal life affects your job performance, the more healthy you and your family can be in every aspect of life—in health, relational health, emotional health, and so on—the more productive you will be at work, and the greater the yield, the dividend, the profit.

Chapter 15

Personal Growth

A strategic prayer partnership propels your personal development.

When you partner with intercessors, you will grow spiritually.

Using the language of gardening, the prayer partnership helps to create fertile soil for your heart so you yield a greater harvest.

Prayer acts like an organic superfood that nourishes the plants for faster growth, and also like a good weeding system that removes the pressure. And it helps to build the overall health of the system, so you are able to resist attacks from the enemy.

When you have the prayer coverage you need, you have the strength to fight your personal and professional battles, and you are well prepared for the future.

Before my family hired Bob as an intercessor, I felt like she was in a football game, trying to carry the football to the end zone, while also fulfilling all the other roles of the offensive line.

But it's really hard to carry the ball anywhere when you're constantly being tackled.

Bob's prayers became my offensive line.

I still had an enormous role to play. No wide receiver thinks, "I do hardly anything in this game."

I still needed skill and speed and focus to carry the vision forward.

But it's so much easier to move forward when someone else blocks the attacks.

Chapter 16

Enlarged Capacity

Through prayer, not only are you more stable and strong in the midst of a crisis, but a strategic prayer partnership also prepares you for future expansion.

You grow, and you prepare for even more growth.

When you pray, and when others pray for you, you start to dream new dreams and experience new capacity.

Bob once bought tomato plants for his children and himself.

After some weeks, his children couldn't believe how much smaller their tomato plants were, compared to his tomato plants.

They all used the same natural fertilizer. They all shared the same weather.

The children had their tomatoes in nice clay pots.

But Bob's tomato plants were in pots that were twice as large, and because of that, his plants were twice as large.

The pot made the difference.

The capacity makes a difference.

Think of Nehemiah. In the book that bears his name, we read of how he served as cupbearer to the king, a trustworthy friend. He was like a small straw that allowed God's grace to flow through him into the palace of the king. He had been content and comfortable in the palace.

But when Nehemiah heard the distressing news of the broken walls around Jerusalem, he had a greater vision, and needed greater capacity. His one-man straw was not enough.

For four months he prayed, crying out to God.

Then the king commissioned him and gave him all the supplies needed to rebuild the walls.

And this took less than two months.

Through prayer, his capacity increased, until he was like an enormous pipe of God's grace, large enough to flood an entire broken city with healing and restoration.

Amazing and inspiring.

Intensive prayer prepared the way for future breakthrough.

Do you feel maxed out, like you have no margin?

Or maybe you're keeping all the balls in the air, but you know that if someone adds one more, everything will come crashing down.

Or maybe you find that you're reacting in anger too much, because you're constantly on edge.

Or you wake up weary and go to bed exhausted.

Many people feel maxed out. When that happens, they have no space for more growth.

Prayer shifts things so that you find ways to have more margin, so that you have new oil to reduce the friction in relationships.

When you have prayer partnership, you'll find that, like helium in a balloon, you sense a lift in your spirit. You'll walk in an atmosphere of hope around you.

A strategic prayer partnership enlarges your capacity for increased growth.

Chapter 17

Triumph Over the Enemy

A strategic prayer partnership is a force of faith, a force of hope, that rewrites the storyline of your life in a positive, life-giving way.

As Christians, we understand that we are engaged in a spiritual battle.

In the Old Testament, we read story after story of the Israelites facing enemy armies that vastly outnumbered them, but when God would fight on their behalf, the Israelites would win.

In the New Testament, Paul wrote in Ephesians 6 and in II Corinthians 10 that we don't battle according to what we see, but against the unseen spiritual forces of wickedness.

The true enemy is not found in other people, but against the principalities and powers.

Prayer rewrites the storyline in a positive, life-giving way.

It's like prayer is the can opener to unlimited possibilities.

Prayer brings the power of breakthrough into your business and your life.

Chapter 18

The One Word to Rule Them All

How to sum up all the benefits of prayer into one word?

Favor.

Prayer increases favor.

Look at these beautiful passages from the Old and New Testaments.

• Numbers 6:24-26: The Lord bless you and keep you; the Lord make his face shine on you and be gracious to you; the Lord turn his face toward you and give you peace.

• Psalm 5:12: Surely, Lord, you bless the righteous; you surround them with your favor as with a shield.

• Luke 2:40: And the child grew and became strong; he was filled with wisdom, and the grace of God was on him.

• Luke 2:52: And Jesus grew in wisdom and stature, and in favor with God and man.

Spiritual growth that adds favor: favor with God and favor with others.

Prayer partnership accelerates this favor, like a rocket booster to launch you out of the area of limitations, obstacles, and hurdles.

Prayer triggers supernatural help for you from heaven's resources.

The promises—the results!—of intercession so far outweigh the cost, it's almost laughable.

Prayer brings results, as God responds to and answers prayer.

Our Clients

Chapter 19

Our Clients

Workplace Prayer Clients

We love our clients! Here's a look at who hires us.

• While most of them are **business owners**, we have a few **employees** who want the kingdom of God to come through them into their place of work, and several people in **ministries** or **nonprofits**. We even have some **families**, who simply want more of the goodness of God. So good!

• We have several **solopreneurs**, and even one who went back to school, not sure of the next step in life, but ready to hear from God. On the opposite end of the spectrum, we have a founder of a 5,500 person organization, and a client who worked as an executive at **one of the Big Four**, before he was poached for his genius and his skills.

• While most **pay for themselves**, we also have a few who **sponsor other organizations** that are dear to them. So beautiful!

• Many are **strong Christians** who have walked with God for decades. At least one came to us after a life of being angry with God, but **curious** to see if that anger could dissipate a bit. And one client, for a season, sponsored a business whose owner didn't show much interest in following Jesus. God blesses them all!

• We have some who are **launching a start-up** and want prayer coverage from the beginning. On the other end, we have **a third generation business** that started back in the early 1970s. And God cares about each!

• We have some clients who are on their **first business venture**, and also **serial entrepreneurs** who start and sell businesses as a matter of course.

• While most clients ask us to pray for their **main work**, we also have clients who work a day job and want us to pray for their **side hustle**. How awesome is that!

• We have **young clients**, **middle aged clients**, and **clients who are close to retirement** and looking at transitions between current management and future management. Celebrate!

• And, in preparing this message, I was stunned to realize that we have at least one representative from **each of the Seven Spheres of Influence**: 1) Education, 2) Religion, 3) Family, 4) Business, 5) Government/Military, 6) Arts/Entertainment, and 7) Media. So thrilled!

So really, there's a place for everyone who wants prayer coverage.

Chapter 20

Three Broad Categories

When we started Workplace Prayer, Bob and I were curious to see who would partner with us.

A few years in, we noticed three general categories.

1) Some clients come in deep distress. A toxic work environment. Extreme fatigue. Hanging on by the fingernails.

Not usually financial distress, but deeper challenges related to staff or poor company culture.

These clients needed immediate triage. They are absolutely desperate for a shift.

2) Some clients are fighting an anaconda. Their businesses are puttering along, but something keeps their real progress choked off.

Staff in the wrong roles? Hidden challenges that would come to light with more focus of prayer? Constant, petty irritations that left them feeling pecked to death by ducks?

These clients needed strengthening and encouraging, as their bigger dreams have been delayed too long.

3) We also have clients who were doing pretty well, but want more. More influence, more kingdom advance, more community transformation.

These clients need the Lord's vision for any pivot to the next thing for their greater impact or legacy.

The same verse in prayer applies to all: Bob loves to pray his life verse, Ephesians 1:17, over all. "I keep asking that the God of our Lord Jesus Christ, the glorious Father, may give you the Spirit of wisdom and revelation, so that you may know him better."

Chapter 21

Who Shouldn't Partner with Us

Now that we have a few years of experience praying for businesses, we've noticed a few red flags from potential partners, indicators that we might not be the right fit in this season.

• Workplace Prayer is not a Hail Mary pass.

In general, we recommend that if a potential client is in a tight spot financially, that they hold off from partnering with us.

While it would be lovely if a business in deep trouble could pay $100 to prayer experts and have a miraculous turnaround in one month ... that isn't what we've seen.

Not saying it won't ever happen, but we haven't seen it yet.

If a business doesn't have sound fundamentals, prayer might help soothe the demise of a business, but thus far, we haven't seen that $100 a month will make an unsound business to be sound.

• Don't go into debt to pay for Workplace Prayer.

While we do have some clients who give sacrificially to be part of Workplace Prayer—and we honor the widow's mite nature of their partnership—we don't believe it's good stewardship to dig a deeper hole in order to have prayer coverage.

If you find yourself in debt, be released to not move forward with us until you reach a more stable financial footing.

• We appreciate when our clients pay us.

As one friend said, "We are spending the time covering you in prayer daily. We appreciate when our clients honor our commitment."

We make payment as easy as possible. We have the option for recurring payments. We are happy to send invoices.

Our clients can choose whether to pay either as a charitable donation, or as a for-profit business expense—we're set up for both.

Common
Objections

Chapter 22

Common Objections

One of the biggest objections is simply whether or not it's okay to pay for prayer. We cover that in a separate short book, *The Ethics of Paying for Prayer*. It covers what the scripture says, along with some other questions and concerns. But here are a few other objections we hear at times.

Chapter 23

Are You Part of the Prosperity Gospel?

A friend asked, "Do you pray for increase? Because I don't think I want to be part of the prosperity gospel."

What a great question!

When we look at the life of the Apostle Paul, clearly he didn't jet around the world. Whipped, beaten with rods, shipwrecked ... so intense.

Or the life of Jesus! Crucifixion!

Their lives demonstrate the opposite of the prosperity gospel.

But one month the Lord invited me to read through the book of Proverbs, and actually trace the benefits that come to the wise person.

Over and over we find that favor follows the righteous, that Wisdom walks with the person who welcomes her.

Three months after hiring Bob, my mom said to me, "Amy, we have been in business for 30 years. We have prayed for our clients, prayed for our products, prayed for our staff, prayed for the delivery drivers. Everything possible we could think of, we've prayed for.

"But we never thought to pray for increase. We are actually doing good in the world! We're seeking to bring God's kingdom! Why would I not want my brand and my products to spread to the places where they're needed?"

The challenge, then, is to hold in tension both the record of history (Jesus, Stephen, Paul, martyrs, etc.), but also hold fast to the promise of the scripture. To actually believe what the Bible says about favor over the righteous. To trust that our businesses succeed as they are doing good in the world.

John, who rested his head on Jesus' breast, wrote in III John 2: "Beloved, I pray that in all respects you may prosper and be in good health, just as your soul prospers."[1]

One client came to us. He said, "I'm in my 50s. I've pretty much hated God my whole life, because of a lot of really hard things in my childhood. But I'm willing to give God a second chance now."

He came expecting the prosperity train.

But instead, he first got right with God.

---

1. LSB

The scriptures started to speak to him. (I got teary the first time he prayed on a call: "I just read Proverbs 3:5-6, and I think this applies to me! *Trust in the Lord with all your heart and lean not on your own understanding; in all your ways submit to him, and he will make your paths straight.*")

His home, that had been a place of conflict, became a place of peace.

He started to do the inner work needed, so that he would be able to handle financial increase.

I wish prayer coverage would allow us all to avoid any kind of pain or difficulty.

It doesn't.

Pain is part of life.

But even with pain, we ask for increase. We want the Lord's hand to be on us, in ever-increasing measure.

Chapter 24

I Still Face Set-Backs

When marketing expert Perry Marshall suggested I hire an intercessor in the fall of 2019, he had already had a paid intercessor for the last decade or so.

A few years after he hired an intercessor, he made a costly business decision. Years of financial setbacks.

He also hired a team member that made some decisions that were extremely costly—almost incalculably costly.[1]

But he didn't say, "Well, clearly, having an intercessor was a poor choice. I'm out."

Instead, he took a principled approach: "I value prayer, and believe that prayer for my business is good, whether this month is up or down."

---

1. For those in the marketing space: he went from the first page of Google to blacklisted.

A decade in, despite some of these costly decisions and challenges, those decisions did not sink him.

They could have, but they didn't.

As one of my friends said: "Perhaps things would have been much worse for Perry had he not had an intercessor!"

In any case, when I look at the impressive things that Perry has been able to accomplish over the last 10 years—in the realm of scientific thought, and cancer research—and when I look ahead at what he most likely will be able to accomplish over the next 10 years, the overall guidance of the Lord is very evident.

Even if sometimes the decisions weren't ideal, and his direction wasn't perfect.

He said, "One of the ways that I know that intercession works is that lucky breaks happen to me that really I have no business having happen. The different connections, the different ideas, the different unexpected breakthroughs."

Which is also to say: the return on investment isn't always immediate.

I offer this to you, because I personally would love it if prayer kept me from all poor decisions and all mistakes.

But I don't think that's quite how prayer works.

Instead, God, as the great restorer, Lord redeems our lives, even in any mistakes we make.

"You've gone into my future to prepare the way, and in kindness you follow behind me to spare me from the harm of my past. You have laid your hand on me!"[2]

2. Psalm 139:5 TPT

Chapter 25

Is It Okay to Outsource Prayer?

My friend Kristin explained that businesses choose to outsource an aspect of their business when that aspect requires specialized knowledge and is outside of their core competency.[1]

Most small businesses have a core competency—tree service, consulting—but hire an accountant to do the taxes.

Specialized knowledge, outside of core competency.

A tech firm that wants to provide meals to its employees would usually be better off outsourcing than trying to hire cafeteria workers to prepare lunches for everyone. The catering services focus on their strengths, and let the tech firm focus on theirs.

---

1. We cover this topic and others at greater length in our booklet *But Can't Anybody Pray?*

Specialized knowledge, outside of core competency.

Effective prayer coverage requires some specialized knowledge, and most businesses aren't dedicated to prayer as their primary task. They have goods to manufacture, or services to render.

To partner with people who are dedicated to prayer makes as much sense as partnering with a CPA for taxes, or a lawn service for property maintenance.

I look at Bob, who has spent 40 years praying and saying, "Lord, teach me to pray." Prayer is the consuming passion of his life.

I've never met anyone else like that.

Some people don't find an hour with God to be a burden, but a starting point. This is a gift of prayer, a calling and vocation from God.

But, of course, "outsourcing" doesn't mean "entire abdication."

Each of us have the privilege to engage with the God of the universe.

If I hired a food service for lunch, I would still need to deal with breakfast, snacks, and dinner. I would need to make sure I didn't mindlessly consume whatever was set in front of me, but avoided allergens and kept the proper portion size.

In the realm of taxes, I still have to provide our accountant with financial statements, and I need to review her work before submitting.

But in the area of business, we want to free businesses to focus on their core competencies.

We still encourage our clients to pray, though! And we have resources to help!

Our Two Main Goals

Chapter 26

Our Two Main Goals

At Workplace Prayer, we focus on two main things, every day.

1) We pray for businesses.

This satisfies the need I felt before I found Bob Perry. I had a business, my family had a business, we prayed over the business, and we had staff pray over the business.

But I felt like we were trying to water a field with a small hose. We might finish eventually, but I wanted to water the field faster.

Could I get a sprinkler system? Or a fire hose?

A trained intercessor offers that fire hose.

When we added a paid intercessor who was trained and powerful ... that was a different story entirely.

2) We train people to pray effectively.

Not just business people, but anyone.

I want to raise up more Bob Perrys.

An intercessor stands in the gap, bringing the stability of heaven to the shakiness of earth. A prayer warrior, if you will. One who intervenes on behalf of another in prayer.

When I didn't have enough training, I faced resistance in prayer. It scared me enough that I more-or-less quit praying for eight years or so.

We have an adversary who, like a roaring lion, roams about seeking whom he may devour, an adversary who comes to steal, kill, and destroy.[1]

He has a plan against us.

We need to be equipped to handle the adversary with wisdom and authority.

When a person of prayer is not aware of how to ensure protection—when a person of prayer is not aware of how to offload the weight that they carry—then the burden becomes too heavy.

But that's the negative side.

The positive side is that we have a Father who loves us with abandon.

Jesus came that we might have *life*, and have it *abundantly*.

We should be able to walk in the joy of the Lord, as the joy of the Lord is our strength; as the kingdom of God is righteousness, peace, and joy in the Holy Spirit.

---

1. John 10:10

When we are not walking in joy, then we are not walking in the fullness that the Lord offers to us.

We want people of prayer to bring life, joy, and hope to their world. We want them to know how to withstand the fiery arrows of the evil one. We want people to be trained to be able to intercede for themselves and, potentially, for businesses effectively and in good health.

What a privilege that, at any time, we are allowed to come to the throne of God, and seek his face on behalf of the work that we're doing.

Let's do so more effectively and strategically.

As such, we have certain prayer resources available to all.

Chapter 27

Daily Encouragement in Your Inbox

S ince March 2020, months before founding Workplace Prayer, I started sending out daily emails about prayer.

At one point, I was tempted to quit, but then realized: so many Workplace Prayer clients read these emails and occasionally say things like, "This was so helpful—all Workplace Prayer clients get these, right?"

Or, "I'm amazed by how often your emails speak into something specific in my life right then."

To get on this list, you can opt-in at praybig.me/email

Sample email below.

Surprising New Thoughts on Traveling

I was planning for a trip at one point, and I had a couple of different options for lodging. One was a very inexpensive, dormitory-style, sleeping arrangement. Or I could get a hotel, which was a good bit more expensive.

But as I thought about these two options, I realized that the dormitory style option was making me feel panicky: no place of my own, no place of safety for my things, some requirement to engage with other people, and especially all of those different emotional and spiritual elements in my personal space.

Once I realized that I was panicky about lodging, it made the decision easy.

Later I was talking this over with Bob, and he said that he has one friend with a wonderful house that could be used as an Airbnb, and yet they choose to let it sit empty most of the time, because the wife is sensitive and doesn't want whatever spiritual cling-ons people might bring into her space.

And he has another friend who bought a motorhome, because when they travel, his wife is so exquisitely sensitive, that she cannot handle staying in hotels. The motorhome is better and easier for her, to simply be in her own space, rather than in other people's environments.

Then I remembered that when my husband and I first finished building our little house, my sister came and stayed during the first nights that we were sleeping in the new house. It didn't yet have indoor plumbing, it didn't have a handle on the door (but it had a very handy towel). But we were inside.

She said, "The space feels so clean, so filled with possibility."

I offer this to you, I suppose, as a statement or a plea for understanding and kindness. If you or a family member have nightmares when you travel, or grow agitated, I used to assume this was because all the normal coping mechanisms vanished, so people (including me) were out of whack.

But maybe that idea is too simplistic. I suspect there's more going on.

A toast to all the sensitive ones: this is part of the gift mix that we carry.

Lord, I ask that you would teach us to use our sensitivity for intercession, that we walk out our unique giftings with you. Thank you, Jesus. Amen.

May we live for the praise of his glory,

Amy Joy

P.S. A few years ago, I wanted to create prayer instruction for people with almost no prayer background at all. Single sentence prayers for the beginner; refresher prayers for the faithful.

If you're looking for how to start thinking about prayer, this is my favorite resource:

Chapter 28

Weekly Prayers in Your Inbox

For years now, Bob has sent out a weekly prayer.

On Mondays, we send out his Workplace Family blessing.

But on Wednesdays, he sends out a more general prayer email. Sometimes he starts with a short teaching before starting to pray.

I like these messages because I feel like Bob is giving me a tutorial in how to pray and what to pray for or about.

To get on this list, sign up here: praybig.me/prayer

Sample email.

Praise Your Way To Breakthrough

Friend,

Do you need God to make a way out of your hardship?

I grew up as a complainer. As a child, moodiness was ordinary behavior in my house, so I learned to follow the pattern, and would be a grouch if circumstances didn't go my way.

When I became a believer as a young adult, I read about the men and women in scripture who praised God, no matter what. That was a very different perspective for me.

When I read about Paul and Silas, who praised God after a beating, I wrote in my journal, "**The power of your praise will determine the magnitude of your breakthrough**."

Acts 16:25, 26 says, "Around midnight Paul and Silas were praying and singing hymns to God, and the other prisoners were listening. Suddenly, there was a massive earthquake, and the prison was shaken to its foundations. All the doors immediately flew open, and the chains of every prisoner fell off!"

When Paul and Silas praised God, God showed up, shook the prison, and set them free.

So, friend, let's praise.

Jesus, we love you! We praise you! We trust you.

Lord, we are not waiting for the breakthrough to come for us to praise and thank you. We praise you as Alpha and Omega, the Beginning and the End. Amid our circumstances, we praise you as Creator.

We adore your name! We praise your character, for you are our God.

You are our Shepherd.

You are our Lord.

You are our Peace.

You are our Supplier.

You are our Healer.

You are our Provider.

You are our Waymaker.

You are our Sanctifier.

You are our Righteousness

You are our Banner of Love.

You are our Master and Friend.

You are our Abiding Presence.

We thank you, Almighty God, for your goodness. Thank you that praise stops the enemy and moves the hand of God. Amen.

To God be the glory,

Bob

Chapter 29

The Make Prayer Beautiful Podcast

After Brian Robinson interviewed me on his Real Faith Stories podcast (praybig.biz/realfaithstories), I realized I had more stories to share.

And so the Make Prayer Beautiful podcast began.

The Make Prayer Beautiful podcast has short episodes, mostly 5-10 minutes long, on what I'm thinking about or learning about in prayer, or stories about prayer, answered questions about prayer.

At first I tried to be very professional, and drove to an empty parking lot and rolled up all my windows to give as silent an environment as possible. As I finished my first recording, a garbage truck drove up behind me.

I have been to that parking lot probably 100 times, and that had never happened before.

I took it as a sign, and so I record them as I go: usually on a prayer walk, but also occasionally when I'm driving. Sometimes I have leaves or snow crunching underfoot. Sometimes I have bird calls in the background.

It's a "come with me as we go" podcast.

praybig.me/podcast

Some Workplace Prayer clients listen occasionally. (I send an email on Friday afternoon with a summary statement of each episode, for those who want occasional listening.)

And some listen faithfully, as a shot of joy or enthusiasm.

You are welcome, too.

Chapter 30

Annual Calendar

P art of our passion at Workplace Prayer is to develop a culture of prayer for any of our clients, and all who are interested.

None of this is required—we are praying regardless!—but we have an annual calendar of Prayer Experiences, beautiful opportunities to grow in prayer throughout the year.

Annual Prayer Experiences

• *January*: F(e)ast: 21 days of prayer and fasting (not necessarily water-only!) to consecrate the year to the Lord; see happybooks.me/feast

• *June*: Seek for Glory: 30 days to pray the prayer of Jabez (just a few minutes a day to radical transformation); see happybooks.me/glory

• *June 19*: Juneteenth Fast: a one-day fast (not necessarily water-only) to help change the narrative to racial reconciliation; see happybooks.me/juneteenth

• *August*: Pursue: 21 days of focused prayer, to help re-set for the second semester of the year; see happybooks.me/pursue

• *October*: Savor Communion: a 31 day emphasis on communion: partake daily, or as often as you feel led; see

happybooks.me/savor

Conclusion: The Bigger Vision

We absolutely love business.

Business offers solutions to the problems God's children face.

In the book of Jeremiah, the Lord gave a message to Jeremiah for the exiles in Babylon: "But seek the welfare of the city where I have sent you into exile, and pray to the LORD on its behalf, for in its welfare you will find your welfare."[1]

The word "welfare" is the word "shalom," also translated "peace" or "wholeness."

Seek the peace, the wholeness, the welfare of the city, for in the peace of the city, you have your peace.

In the wholeness of the city, you have your wholeness.

In the right alignment of the city, you have your right alignment.

---

1. Jeremiah 29:7 ESV

One of the reasons that the Workplace Prayer team loves praying for businesses is that when businesses thrive, their cities thrive, too.

Before we formed Workplace Prayer, Stoll Industries noticed that their county, Abbeville, South Carolina, was going backwards in every measurable way.

- Higher rates of addiction
- Higher rates of divorce
- Greater poverty
- Greater unemployment
- Lower graduation rates
- Lower property values

They thought, "This ought not be! As a Christian company in the midst of this county, we need to address this!"

Shortly afterward they hired Bob Perry, among others, to pray. They established a prayer house. They prayerwalked their city.

And they have started to see a shift.

Client and friend Paul Van Hoesen first went to Stoll in 2019. Four years later, in the spring of 2023, he returned. He wrote to Bob and me:

ele

As a testament to all your prayer work here: I worked in rural economic development for Tennessee. I've been in A LOT of rural towns and villages, and what is typically on them isn't good spiritually.

Abbeville feels clean, bright, alive, industrious, healthy in the Spirit.

Mary J noticed it when we drove to the grocery last night. It was dark, she couldn't see much, but it could be felt.

It did not feel like this when I was last here in 2019!

Well done, good and faithful servants! Your talent multiplied!

———— *ell* ————

Businesses that pray can see thriving cities.

What a satisfying vision.

Thank you for acting for the welfare not only of yourself, but for the city around you.

Lord, thank you that you invite all of us to peace, as an act of goodwill that extends out. What an invitation. Thank you, Jesus.

Your word says: "To those who by perseverance in doing good seek glory, honor, and immortality, He will give eternal life."[2]

May we seek that glory, honor, and immortality!

You created us to do amazing and glorious things! May we go for it and not hold back!

Amen.

---

2. Romans 2:7

An Invitation

Who Is Praying for You and Your Business?

I was once talking to a friend. He told me about a conversation with one of his clients, who had hired young prostitutes in Las Vegas.

My friend said, "Why are you doing that? They are the age of your daughter!"

The client replied, "That's what makes it good."

I looked at my friend, stunned. I had no idea this was part of his workday ... or anyone's workday.

I had researched trafficking, and understood the importance of rescuing those who daily face betrayal and abuse.

But to minister to those who abuse? To call the client to a better life, and to face such an unbelievable and horrific response?

"Who is covering you in prayer when you go into the pit of hell like that?"

"I have some friends who pray for me."

"Do they pray more than one sentence a week?"

"Uh ... what is that you do again?"

Hopefully you are not dealing with anything quite so blatantly exploitive and wicked. His example is extreme.

But all of us in the workplace deal with challenges every day. We need:

• Direction

• Wisdom

• Easing of relationships between staff members

• Legal protection

• Energy and strength for the journey

On and on....

So I ask you the same question I asked my friend: *who is covering you and your business in prayer?*

At Workplace Prayer, this is what we do, all day, every day.

Appendices

A Few Testimonies

"I Want Change, and I Want It Now"

A month after Shane and Ronda, owners of Trask Insurance, partnered with us, we asked, "Why did you hire Workplace Prayer?"

And mild-mannered Shane pounded his fist on the table and said, "I want change, and I want it now!"

That conversation was on March 11, or 3/11.

On June 22, or 6/22—that original date, doubled—Trask Insurance closed their biggest account ever.

But that wasn't all. Shane looked around that day and realized: in the last three months, his family had a new house drop into their lap. They weren't expecting that.

And they'd bought another office. They hadn't seen that coming.

And this was in a year of global upheaval, 2021.

But for Shane and his family, it was an exciting year.

Shane said later:

When I started with Workplace Prayer, I did a kind of an intake form, and I had a whole list of things to pray for: for the community, for our office, for our family.

And each one of them felt like Mount Everest, like wow, there's no way I can do that on my own.

Some of them were dreams I'd had for ten years and more, that I had seen no real movement on.

That list I'd made: it was like God used it as a checklist: yes, yes, yes, yes, yes.

And then he gave even more!

Now we're praying for the revival that begins in the desert of Washington that will spread to Olympia, the capital of Washington.

With Shane and Ronda, we stand in awe of what God can do.

Dream big! Ask big! He does more than we can ask or imagine![1]

The Holy Spirit as the HR Department

After farmers Gilbert and Kirsten hired Workplace Prayer, Kirsten told us the backstory.

> We had an HR girl for a year or two. We paid her nice salary every month. And every month she did reports and came back and offered the reports about what was happening.
>
> But after we did this, month after month, we realized that she had no ability to actually implement change. She just reported the data.
>
> Finally I looked at Gilbert and said, "Should we invite the Holy Spirit to be our HR department?"
>
> "Well, we could kick over the stone, and see what's under there."

And so they gave it a try.

Within the first two months of hiring Workplace Prayer, they had replaced their farm manager of several years with an internal promotion.

The new farm manager proved to be so spectacularly good in his new role that many of the challenges around the farm simply vanished.

With the right person in place, they no longer had any need for regular reports on how the team could work together better.

As Kirsten said: "There is such a glory on the farm."

Everything works better with the Holy Spirit's help.

ele

No Longer Alone

Workplace Prayer client Chris came to us in December 2020. He had hated God most of his life, but was willing to explore what it might look like to not hate God.

Four months later, in early April 2021, he shared what had happened so far.

ele

Most of my life, I've had a very stubborn, Irish-Scotch prideful certainty that I knew best for me. So everything else, including God, including the Bible, could just stay away.

But one day I heard marketing expert Perry Marshall say that he had a paid intercessor, and I asked him, "I don't know what intercessors are, and why would you use one? What are these intercessors?"

He connected me to Workplace Prayer.

Then I was on the first Zoom call, and I almost went running because I was thought, "Okay, this sounds like some kind of 1800s revival thing here. I've got to go."

But I stuck it out through that first meeting. And it really opened so much for me.

Now one of the first things I asked for was a revenue explosion, and to consistently grow and blah, blah, blah.

And I didn't get any of that. At first I was little confused.

But you know what I got? I got what I really needed.

First, the spiritual transformation. Because, to be honest, I don't think I was really ever in a spiritual place to responsibly handle the kind of success and impact that I want to have. But I never knew that until recently.

I also prayed for an increase in productivity and focus. And I feel like I've become 500% more focused and productive. I'm really not exaggerating. I have so much more clarity now that I feel like a different person.

I'm not torn in three or four or five different ways.

I do my prayer time every morning, which I've never done before. And the clarity keeps increasing.

And when I work out with swimming, instead of just jamming tunes, I'm communing with with God, back and forth.

It used to be so boring, going back and forth. But now it's actually quite great. It's great time alone to pray through movement.

You know, I've also prayed for family peace. We have had so much contention for years and years. There have been a few points where I felt like, "I'm just going to leave. I cannot stand this." But the thing that kept me were the kids.

But I'm finding myself becoming more patient with stuff that used to drive me up the wall. Now it might be a little irritating. But it's not actually that bad. I can deal with this.

So there's just so much transformation.

And a really huge one is I don't feel alone anymore.

That's probably the biggest.

Before I was operating like I had to do everything myself, figure it out myself.

And now I feel like I'm like never, ever alone. And that's just mind blowing.

Because that aloneness goes back as far as I can remember.

I love Workplace Prayer. Amy and Bob, thank you so much for all that you do. This is just profoundly amazing. And that's it. Thank you.[2]

---

2. A few months after this testimony, Chris was on the Real Faith Stories podcast. We absolutely rejoiced at what he shared. Need a bit of encouragement? So good! https://praybig.biz/chris

A Few Client Call-Outs

A Happy Shout-Out on LinkedIn

On May 5, 2023, I posted my first ever LinkedIn article. (Please feel free to connect with me!)

Client, friend, and mentor Paul Van Hoesen wrote a beautiful recommendation in response.

> If you are wanting God's purpose truly fulfilled in your business and in your own life as an owner/partner, dedicated and intentional intercession is essential.
>
> Intercession is the missing spiritual dimension in business that is becoming more essential as the complexity of the marketplace increases.
>
> I have been a founding client of Workplace Prayer with Bob and Amy and the impact their teams have had on my personal life and my business ventures has been well worth the price. I'm

a believer!

Businesses spend the money to hire a solid marketing agency because they understand the power of good marketing in sales.

If you truly understand the power of prayer and the impact of having your business aligned with Kingdom of God, a Workplace Prayer team inside your company is worth every penny. Shalom!

You Don't Have to Convince Me; I'm Already Sold

Clients Lane and Denise run a CPA firm.

The first time I talked to Denise about Workplace Prayer, she said, "You don't have to convince me; I'm already sold."

And I said, "Wait ... what?! That's not normal. Most people at least have some questions! Tell me more about that!"

She said:

> I know firsthand the power of prayer. My husband and I are lay pastors at our church, which basically means that we don't get paid. I have learned that if somebody asks, "Will you pray about this?" to say, "Oh, yes! I will pray right now."
>
> And after I pray, I might not think about it again.

I recognize that what you're offering takes discipline and time. It's a worthy offering, because you're being fruitful. You're offering fruitfulness to others. There's that scripture, "Don't muzzle the ox when it's treading the grain."
You're providing fruitfulness for those you pray for, and we get to take part in that.
There is nothing evil about money!
In fact, I *cherish*—no, that word is not even strong enough a word—but I *cherish* the thought of my family being prayed over, and our business being prayed over."

I loved this conversation, because I, too, cherish the thought of my family and my business being prayed over.

I'm an intercessor, but my husband's business and my business are also clients of Workplace Prayer.

Bob, too, is a client.

Because we, too, cherish the prayer coverage.

———*ele*———

A Surprising Benefit of a Prayer Agreement

In 2021, I met with our client Emma in person for the first time.

Over dinner, we had a surprising—and, for me, eye-opening—conversation around charging for prayer.

"If you didn't charge for prayer, first of all, I would have a problem. It would be hard for me to rely on you as much as I do because I would feel guilty: here are these incredible intercessors who pray with Michael W. Smith and sports teams and famous people. And here I am demanding their time.

"But the fact that I pay for it releases me from any feeling of guilt or fear, or, 'Oh gosh, am I bothering them?'

"It's like, no, this is a service we pay for, so it actually makes it really easy not just to ask, but to ask often. And in fact, most of the time the guilt I have is that I'm not giving you enough information. I'm not feeding back to you enough just how effective this has been."[1]

So interesting to me! New language to try to talk about what we do.

---

1. Though, yes, Bob has done several initiatives with Michael W. Smith, and prayed for the Washington football team (back when they were still the Redskins), prayerwalked through all the floors of Air Force One, led prayer for the Final Four, among other assignments, he really just loves to pray. No need to feel guilty for asking for prayer!

The Sonlight List

A Celebration of the Goodness of God at Sonlight

Spiritual Blessings

1. Daily prayer for the unreached and the needs of the customers

2. Staff that prays

3. Staff spiritual transformation over time—we celebrate the baby steps

4. Replaced two A to Z prayer books for unreached people groups, because the people groups included were no longer unreached

5. Many missionaries able to stay on the field one more year, without sending children to boarding school

6. Fundraisers for the unreached: raise awareness and impact of children; $1.5 million raised

7. The opportunity to connect ministries that weren't connected before

8. Millions available for missions: $15 million+

9. A company that seeks to always be conciliatory and kind; demonstration of Christian principles and ethics in conduct-

ing ourselves (example: one year we replaced all language arts because we thought customers deserved to have a better package)

10. Children receive a solid, biblical education

———*ell*———

Educational Blessings

11. Several hundred thousand children who love to learn

12. Scholarship applications: always a treat to see the phenomenal and astounding young people and their accomplishments

13. Students claim, "I'm a voracious reader," or, "We bought more than one program because only one program didn't have enough books": unique in the educational world

14. Sonlight grad now working at Sonlight

15. Able to keep good books in print—some books have made it all 30 years

16. Competent, qualified grads who go out to change the world

17. Hundreds of testimonials: every year, new photos and captions

18. Grateful customers—like the woman who brought Sarita chocolates at a convention

19. Second generation Sonlighters

20. Thousands of books read

21. Children all have favorite book titles (compared to the school system: do children even know the titles of their textbooks?)

22. Wide breadth of careers post-graduation, even with the same books

23. Damaged books: given away to missionaries, to schools: no waste, but we've shared a lot

24. Before Sonlight, there was nothing about literature-rich, but today the world talks about it; the transformation of educational industry

25. Read-Aloud: used to have to define it, now popular

26. Charlotte Mason said, "No twaddle," but we flipped it to a positive: "love to learn"

_____ele_____

Staff-Related Blessings

27. Over 600 employees: don't work weekends, flexible hours, ideal for moms

28. Safety in travel to and from work: only one accident, and though the car was totaled, she walked away in safety and came to work the next day

29. Health for employees: in 30 years, one wife had failing kidneys when her husband came to work at Sonlight; one spouse had cancer when her husband began, but she has been cancer-free for 22 years; one person fell out a window; one

spouse died of cancer; other than these, we have to wrack our brains to think of a life-threatening illness

30. No ugly divorces (and only one total, among all the staff over 30 years)

31. Several employees have worked over 20 years; a longer-than-average duration, and low turnover rate

32. Impact many immigrants

33. Positive impact on temps: many come back and request to work at Sonlight

34. Sonlight moms work as Advisors

35. Sonlight moms attend conventions

36. The opportunity to employ many people, so moms can stay home to care for kids

37. Seeing people develop and grow—staff growth

38. Employees who become US citizens

39. Former employees return to say hello

40. Develop good friendships

41. No vile speech in the work environment

42. Calm and serene environment; a place of peace; contractors, vendors, suppliers comment: "It's so quiet here! Is anyone working?"

—— *ell* ——

Protection Blessings

43. During the August 1997 UPS strike, which would have destroyed our business, and FedEx wasn't taking more cus-

tomers, we realized we had accepted a free mailer some months prior, and so had an account number—provision during this traumatic time

44. Protection for a brand name: though a company with a very different name brought a lawsuit against the name, the Lord provided

45. The name "Sonlight" was once in jeopardy because a Sunday school curriculum also used the title, but, again, the Lord provided

46. In a time of harassment, the staff was able to work through without any negative impact

47. An odd situation with unethical reselling that resolved peaceably

48. Protected in Texas from changing tax laws—this could have devastated our company, but we were spared

49. Protection from a lawsuit by one disgruntled former employee

50. Insurance to cover hacking when one brand was hacked

51. Protected from government enquiry after a wrongful unemployment claim

52. No small business loan, so John didn't have to do invasive financials 4-6 times a year; the Line of Credit was sufficient, and that saved maybe $700,000

Favor and Provision Blessings

53. One of Sarita's friends, in the first year, said, "You know I would love to order every book you have"; then a woman provided money for education for two years, and because Juliet had stair-stepped children and was going on the mission field: she got every book

54. Inexpensive garage as the initial space for the building: $25/month: paid actual costs + $5/week for UPS shipping

55. Efficient, practical, useful building—so convenient, on the bus line (staff prayed over the empty lot)

56. Building on time and under budget

57. Bought the land at a fire sale price: was $5/square foot; but we bought it for $2.73 or $2.71/square foot

58. Built expansion and all the racking with cash while the company was flush with cash

59. Replacement books when a title goes out of print: always find something

60. New bankers: creative and helpful

61. Really good, professional advisors—so many people to collaborate and advise

62. Useful equipment: forklift, solar panels, baler for boxes (saved money—buy back baled cardboard), computers

63. Transition from paper to web business (all reports on paper originally)

64. Launched multiple branches successfully; only one small effort was not, but though we paid for the name, we didn't outlay much money

65. Every time (almost) we bring in an employee: increased competence; upward progression, better employees

66. Early on, an advisor suggested some inexpensive changes, allowing us to stay in a less expensive facility an extra year

67. Always pay our vendors on time, and so set a tone and way for doing business that's upright

68. Empower the customer relations team to actually help people

Sample Weekly Prayer List

2023.10.22-28

Returning

Praise

• I am very full coming back from the Fusion conference. Yesterday I was wiped out, emotionally spent, physically weary. I logged quite a lot of walking miles, didn't get a whole lot of sleep, spent 20 minutes or more solid shaking under the presence of the Holy Spirit, slept in a bed not my own. After a four hour hike today, I am doing ever so much better, and excited to see what the Lord does next.

• I feel a strong invitation from the Lord to ask more and better questions, and to be seeking to live bi-locationally, both seated in the heavenlies with Christ, and also on this earth. What an invitation, to actually press in to see what the Spirit of the Lord is doing in the earth.

• Good, swift dentist appointment up in town.

Prayers

• I have a tremendous lot of unopened emails and files to process, while also wanting to still be absorbing all that I took in. A conference often has an open heaven coming out of it, so I want to get all the goodness of the open heaven that I can.

• I feel a bit like I'm in a snow globe. That I've been picked up, shaken around, and there's a swirl. But I'm not actually sure about the various parts: will some be rearranged, or wiped out? I have no idea. *Your way, Lord.*

Which is, I suppose, a good place to be. Hooray for the liminal space!

About the Authors

When Bob prays, things happen.

Once Bob was going to come to Colorado to help a client with a project. A.J. had been in Colorado already for some weeks, and though the Front Range usually has a beautiful view of the Rocky Mountains, massive wildfires had obscured them entirely the whole time she had been in the state.

At the last minute, Bob wasn't able to come.

But the day that he was scheduled to arrive, the mountains were suddenly clear.

But there hadn't been a rainfall or a snowfall, or a massive windstorm to blow the smoke away.

There was no natural explanation for the suddenly clear view.

Three days later, A.J. mentioned this to him.

He chuckled and said, "Oh, that's because I prayed that the view would be good when I was there."

This is a crazy story, because first of all, Bob didn't even arrive.

Second, because all the Colorado residents suddenly got to enjoy the view of the mountains again, because of Bob's prayer.

Third, because this was (if we're being honest) a frivolous request.

But that's the reality of how God answers Bob's prayers.

Bob is willing to ask for big things, and God likes to say yes.

—ell—

A.J.'s claim to fame in prayer is that she quit praying for eight years because she faced a certain amount of targeted malicious attacks, and it freaked her out so much she couldn't handle it.

So she had almost a decade in her life where Bob's teaching would have been incredibly effective in encouraging her to pray some more.

So if you don't feel like a prayer expert, come and talk to A.J., because she's your girl.

Made in USA - North Chelmsford, MA
76265_9798893500288
02.20.2024 2028